DISCOVER AMERICA'S NATIONAL PARKS

BLACK SOLDIERS IN THE CIVIL WAR

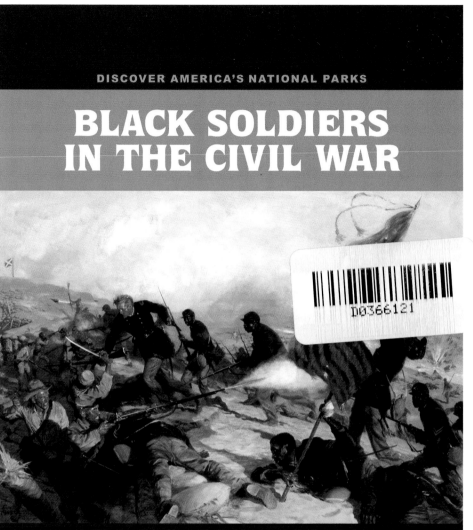

Union army black soldiers attack a Confederate stronghold in South Carolina.

WRITTEN BY RICK BEARD

Copyright 2016 by Eastern National
470 Maryland Drive, Suite 1, Fort Washington, PA 19034
Visit us at www.eParks.com

The America's National Parks Press series is produced by Eastern National, a not-for-profit partner of the National Park Service. Our mission is to promote the public's understanding and support of America's national parks and other public trust partners by providing quality educational experiences, products, and services.

ISBN 978-1-59091-163-1

Once let the black man get upon his person the brass letters U.S., let him get an eagle on his button, and a musket on his shoulder, and bullets in his pocket, and there is no power on earth or under the earth which can deny that he has earned the right of citizenship in the United States.

—Frederick Douglass, "Should the Negro Enlist in the Union Army?"
National Hall, Philadelphia, July 6, 1863

Most historians now agree that slavery was the primary cause of the Civil War. But to the chagrin of Northern abolitionists and black leaders such as Frederick Douglass, Abraham Lincoln and the Union army seemed slow to embrace the destruction of slavery as the primary aim of the conflict and slower still to enlist blacks in the fight. Neither free nor enslaved African Americans displayed any such hesitancy when identifying a Union victory with the end of chattel slavery and volunteering to fight in the effort. "In struggling for their [whites] own nationality," argued an editorial writer in *The Anglo African*, a New York City antislavery weekly, "they are forced to defend our rights."

On the eve of the Civil War, the population of the United States included about 200,000 free and almost 1.6 million enslaved black men between the ages of 15 and 40. By war's end, 178,985 African American men (along with 7,122 white officers) had fought to preserve the Union; another 29,500 had joined the Union navy. It is likely that more than 135,000 of those who served in the United States Colored Troops (USCT) were former slaves, a number arrived at by adding the 41,719 recruits from the Union slave states to the 93,542 recruits from the Confederate slave states. Beginning

Left: Song sheet cover published during the Civil War.

Frederick Douglass

in 1863, units of the USCT fought in 449 engagements, 39 of which were major battles. Sixteen soldiers and four sailors received the Congressional Medal of Honor for their deeds. Over 37,300 died, many of them from disease, and far more suffered from sickness, wounds, and other war-related injuries.

The service of the USCT during the last two years of the war, at a moment when the Union army was in desperate need of reinforcements, played a vital role in the North's eventual triumph. The following interview of an anonymous veteran, recorded during the 1930s by the Federal Writers' Project, succinctly captures why they fought:

"When I went to the War, I was turning seventeen. I was in the Battle of Nashville, when we whipped old Hood. I went to see my mistress on my furlough, and she was glad to see me. She said, 'You remember when you were sick and I had to bring you to the house and nurse you?' And I told her, 'Yes'm, I remember.' And she said, 'And now you are fighting me!' I said, 'No'm, I ain't fighting you. I'm fighting to get free.'"

"This is a white man's war"

At the beginning of the Civil War, few but the most ardent abolitionists advocated arming blacks to help squash the Southern rebellion. In a speech delivered on April 13, 1861, one day after the firing on Fort Sumter, Frederick Douglass, the nation's leading antislavery spokesman, contended that, "Five hundred black men, divided into guerilla bands...can do more to destroy slavery than five thousand Regulars."

Douglass' faith in the prowess of black soldiers was well-placed. Both free and enslaved African American soldiers and sailors had fought valiantly during the Revolutionary War, the undeclared naval war with

France between 1798 and 1800, and the War of 1812. They fought despite determined efforts in the 1790s to prevent their enlistment in state militias or the navy and Marine Corps. In light of this military tradition, it was no surprise when free men and women came forward after Fort Sumter with offers "to stand by and defend the Government with our lives, our fortunes, and our sacred honor." Authorities in cities throughout the North—Boston, Providence, New York, Philadelphia, Cincinnati, Cleveland —rebuffed such expressions of support without exception. In Cincinnati, one police official warned the local African American community to "keep out.... This is a white man's war."

Within days of Douglass' fiery speech, Secretary of War Simon Cameron tersely deflected an offer of "three hundred reliable colored citizens" to help defend Washington during the suspenseful first weeks of the war, when a Confederate assault on the nation's capital city seemed imminent. "This Department has no intention at present," he wrote, "to call into the services of the Government any colored soldiers."

The North's initial resistance to enlisting black troops began to waver in the face of demoralizing defeats at Bull Run in July and Ball's Bluff in October 1861. At the same time, the flood of slaves escaping to Union lines

Fugitive slaves entering Union lines, 1867 painting by Theodor Kaufmann.

Frederick Douglass Visits the White House

On August 10, 1863, Frederick Douglass arrived in Washington, D.C., for the first time. Although he had no appointment, he hoped to meet with President Lincoln to discuss his concerns about black soldiers' inequitable pay, the need for retaliation against Confederate policies toward black troops, and guarantees that black soldiers would be promoted for meritorious service. After meeting briefly with Secretary of War Stanton, who expressed sympathy for his views and offered him a commission in the Union army so that he could continue his recruiting activities, Douglass went to the White House. To his surprise, he was ushered into the president's office almost immediately.

Although Lincoln instantly put Douglass at ease, the abolitionist leader later reported that he was "not entirely satisfied with [the president's] views." Lincoln argued, for instance, that blacks "ought to be willing to enter the service upon any condition," and that lower pay was a "necessary concession to smooth the way." Nonetheless, Douglass left the

Frederick Douglass flanked by black heroes Blanche Kelso Bruce and Hiram Rhodes Revels.

White House "well satisfied with the man," and four months later told an audience in Philadelphia, "I tell you I felt big there!"

The first of Douglass' visits to see Lincoln enhanced his status as a leading voice in the antislavery community.

challenged the Lincoln administration to consider the degree to which slaves might be willing to fight for their freedom. In May, Major General Benjamin Butler coined the term "contraband of war" when refusing to return three escaped slaves to their Virginia owner. The First Confiscation Act, signed three months later, mandated that any property—a term which included enslaved men and women—used to further the Confederate cause could be confiscated. The act carefully described the dual character of slaves as property under state law and persons under the U.S. Constitution. More importantly, the act declared that masters whose slaves were "employed in hostility to the United States" would forfeit their labor; these slaves were emancipated as part of the North's prosecution of the war. Thousands of contrabands continued to come into Union lines, seeking assistance and freedom.

By year's end, Simon Cameron had changed his mind, suggesting in his annual report to Congress that it was "clearly the right of the Government to arm slaves when it may become necessary." Lincoln forced Cameron to remove this recommendation from his report, and within two months replaced him with Edwin Stanton.

"Forever free of their servitude"

The president's rebuke of his secretary of war was the first of many actions he would take to rein in overzealous administration officials and army field commanders eager to enlist blacks in the Union war effort. On May 9, 1862, General David Hunter issued an order emancipating all the slaves in those areas of Georgia, South Carolina, and Florida under his command. He also began organizing a regiment drawn from freedmen on the sea islands of South Carolina. Lincoln quickly revoked Hunter's emancipation order and crushed his and similar attempts to form black military units in southern Louisiana and in Kansas.

But management of the growing contraband population posed a greater challenge than did emancipationist field commanders. As many as

Black dockworkers in Virginia.

500,000 African American men, women, and children eventually found their way to camps established to care for these refugees. Delighted to discover a new labor pool, the Union army quickly tasked them with building fortifications, clearing forests, cooking, planting and harvesting crops on nearby plantations, and completing a host of tasks that might otherwise have fallen to soldiers. Unfortunately, their wages frequently went unpaid, a situation that compounded the army's frequent unwillingness to feed and shelter the laborers' families.

On July 17, 1862, Congress sent Lincoln two acts that would irrevocably redefine the wartime role of African Americans. The Second Confiscation Act declared slaves owned by disloyal masters to be "forever free of their servitude" and reconfirmed an earlier act of Congress that forbade Federal soldiers from returning runaways to their masters. Although the law proved unenforceable, it did provide Union commanders with clear directives for the treatment of runaways. The Militia Act, passed at the same time, paved the way for the recruitment of former slaves as soldiers in the Union army by authorizing Lincoln "to receive into the service... persons of African descent...for the purpose of constructing entrenchments, or performing camp service or any other labor, or any military or naval service."

The Militia Act mandated that "persons of African descent" were to be paid less than white soldiers, a provision that rested on the shaky justification that black troops were to serve as garrison, not front-line, troops. Many Northern opinion makers agreed with an editorial in *The New York World*. "To claim that the indolent, servile negro is the equal in courage, enterprise and fire of the foremost race in all the world is a libel," the paper editorialized. "It is unjust in every way to the white soldier to put him on a level with the black."

"The great available...force for restoring the Union"

In August 1862, the president and his secretary of war took steps to form the first Federally sanctioned black regiments. Lincoln replaced General David Hunter as commander of the Department of the South with General Rufus Saxton, a Medal of Honor winner, and Edwin Stanton immediately authorized him to recruit 5,000 volunteers at Port Royal,

South Carolina. Unfortunately, the usually meticulous Stanton then erred. He dictated that the volunteers were "to be entitled to and receive the same pay and rations as are allowed by law to volunteers in the service," a mistake that would go unnoticed for nine months and once discovered cause untold problems.

These black soldiers in South Carolina were taught to read and write.

Administration policy dictated that only white officers could command black troops, so Saxton tapped Massachusetts abolitionist Thomas Wentworth Higginson to lead the new regiment. He embraced his mission with characteristic zeal and thoroughly drilled the new recruits to prepare them for battle. "The first man who organizes and commands a successful black regiment," he recorded in his journal, "will perform the most important service in the history of the war."

After his troops had performed admirably in a series of small engagements, Higginson suggested that "the fate of the whole movement for colored soldiers rested on the behavior of this one regiment." By the time he wrote these words in May 1863, the "movement for colored soldiers" was well underway. On January 1, 1863, President Lincoln drew upon his executive powers to declare the millions of slaves still under Confederate control "forever free" and announced that former slaves "will be received into the armed service of the United States."

For an army staggering from unprecedented casualties at Shiloh, Antietam, and Fredericksburg, the Emancipation Proclamation was a godsend. Lincoln clearly recognized the importance of black recruitment. "The colored population is the great available and yet unavailed of, force for restoring

A Union soldier reads the Emancipation Proclamation to a black family.

Recruiting Black Troops for the Union

The decision to recruit African Americans as front-line soldiers, codified in the Emancipation Proclamation, came at a favorable moment for a Union army that

This illustration was used to encourage black men to enlist as volunteers in the Union army.

had suffered unprecedented casualties at Shiloh, Antietam, Fredericksburg, and other bloody battles. The creation of the Bureau of Colored Troops in May 1863, soon led to the implementation of regional strategies with which to fill the ranks of the United States Colored Troops.

In the North, the authority to enlist black troops rested with state governments as well as public and private organizations. Recruiting in the Mississippi River Valley and along the Atlantic coast relied on impressment—forcing men into military service. In the border states, the military itself generally oversaw USCT recruiting. Because the Lincoln administration decided that only white officers would command black troops, over 4,000 candidates for appointment as officers in the USCT chose to submit to testing and interviews; approximately 2,400 were commissioned.

Ultimately, 178,975 African Americans filled 133 infantry regiments, four independent companies, seven cavalry regiments, 12 regiments of heavy artillery, and 10 companies of light artillery. Over a third of those men would become casualties of war.

A Union recruitment poster aimed at Northern blacks.

the Union," the president wrote in a March 1863 letter. "The bare sight of fifty thousand armed and drilled black soldiers on the banks of the Mississippi would end the rebellion at once."

Initial efforts at recruiting African Americans were clumsy, scattershot, and often counterproductive until late May, when Stanton created the Bureau of Colored Troops. Major Charles Foster, the Bureau's head, devised different regional recruiting strategies. In New England and the Middle Atlantic, he delegated the authority to enlist black troops to state governments and to public and private organizations such as the Union League in Philadelphia. Resistance among state leaders in the Midwest limited recruiting efforts in that area of the country, while recruiters along the Atlantic coast and in the Mississippi River Valley relied on impressment—forcing military service on men. In the border states and those areas of the Confederacy controlled by Union forces, the military itself generally oversaw recruiting, drawing heavily from the contraband camps.

"Recruits were taken wherever found," recalled one Maryland soldier. "The laborer in the field would throw down his hoe or quit his plow and march away with the guard, leaving his late owner looking after him in speechless amazement." Loyal slaveholders received $300 from the Federal government for each slave who enlisted, an amount well below the existing market value of a slave.

A Union recruiter in Memphis described the transformation undergone by new recruits:

"The average plantation negro was a hard-looking specimen...[in] a close-fitting wool shirt, and pantaloons of homespun material.... The first pass made at him was with a pair of shears.... The next was to strip him of his filthy rags and burn them, and scour him thoroughly with soap and water. A clean new suit of army blue was now put on him, together with a full suite of military accoutrements, and a gun was placed in his hands, and, lo! He was completely metamorphosed."

By the end of October 1863, Foster could report that there were 58 black regiments totaling 37,482 troops in the Union army—a year later, there were 140 black regiments totaling 101,950 troops. And by war's end, a total of 178,975 African Americans were organized into 133 infantry regiments, four independent companies, seven cavalry regiments, 12 regiments of heavy artillery, and 10 companies of light artillery. The Northern free states produced 37,723 recruits, with Pennsylvania (8,612), Ohio (5,092), and New York (4,125) leading the way. Kentucky supplied 57 percent of the 41,719 recruits from the Union slave states. And Louisiana (24,052), Tennessee (20,133), and Mississippi (17,869) supplied more than two-thirds of the 93,542 USCT recruits from the Confederate slave states.

Emancipation Day in South Carolina

On January 1, 1863, slavery's opponents gathered throughout the Union to celebrate the Emancipation Proclamation. The jubilation was nowhere greater than in Port Royal, South Carolina. For Charlotte Forten, a black abolitionist from Philadelphia, "the most glorious day this nation has yet seen" began about 10 am. "The people began to collect by land, and also by water," Colonel Thomas Wentworth Higginson, 1st South Carolina Volunteers wrote, "The multitude were chiefly colored women...and a sprinkling of men...[but] there were white visitors also—ladies on horseback and in carriages, superintendents and teachers, officers and cavalrymen."

The day was filled with speeches, with a "grand barbecue" crowning the event, but the ceremony's highlight was a purely spontaneous outburst of song. "Just as Colonel Higginson advanced to take the flag," one spectator recalled, "a negro woman standing near began to sing 'America,' and soon many voices of freedmen and women joined in the beautiful hymn, and sang it so touchingly that everyone was thrilled beyond measure." Higginson, deeply moved, recalled, "When they stopped, there was nothing to do for it but to speak, and I went on; but the life of the whole day was in those unknown people's song."

A volunteer regiment in South Carolina celebrates the emancipation of slaves.

Union army black soldiers in the trenches during battle.

The increasingly successful effort to recruit colored troops was the first step toward replenishing the Union army's ranks. The selection of white officers to lead the troops came next. In late spring 1863, review boards began meeting regularly in Washington, New Orleans, St. Louis, Davenport, Nashville, and Cincinnati "to examine applicants for commissions to command colored troops." Those volunteering for leadership positions in the USCT voiced a variety of motives—chief among them were sympathy for blacks, a desire to help elevate the race, a commitment to saving the Union, and personal advancement. One New York soldier saw it as the opportunity "to prove that I am what I have always professed to be—an Abolitionist."

Candidates were expected to master tactics, army regulations, general military knowledge, history, geography, and mathematics. The higher the rank sought, the more the candidate was expected to know. One soldier seeking a colonelcy had to answer 293 questions. About 40 percent of candidates were rejected. The high rate of failure prompted a group of Philadelphia Unionists to establish a month-long training program for applicants in December 1863. Over the next nine months, the rigorous program produced 484 graduates. A total of 9,000 white soldiers applied to be officers in the USCT over the course of the last two years of the war. Of the 4,000 who took the exam, about 60 percent received a commission.

Members of Company E, 4th U.S. Colored Infantry, in Washington, D.C.

The success of the Union recruiters mirrored the public's growing comfort with the idea of black troops. "The day for raising a panic over Negro enlistment has passed," wrote Whitelaw Reid in the *Cincinnati Gazette*. Many Union soldiers were increasingly open to accepting black comrades in arms. "A year ago last January I didn't like to hear anything of emancipation," wrote one Illinois soldier in the spring of 1863. "Last fall, [I] accepted confiscation of rebels' Negroes quietly. In January [I] took to emancipation readily, and now...am becoming so [color] blind that I can't see why they will not make soldiers."

Black troops quickly validated the optimism expressed by this Illinois soldier. The early successes of Colonel Higginson's 1st South Carolina Volunteers were repeated at the siege of Port Hudson, and at the Battle of Milliken's Bend on June 7, 1863. In a report to Edwin Stanton, Assistant Secretary of War Charles A. Dana wrote, "The bravery of the blacks in the battle at Milliken's Bend completely revolutionized the sentiment of the army with regard to the employment of negro troops."

In August 1863, Lincoln articulated the political agreement implicit

The Assault on Fort Wagner

At dusk on July 18, 1863, the 54th Massachusetts, a regiment of black infantry commanded by Colonel Robert Gould Shaw, led the second assault in a week against Fort Wagner. Well positioned on Morris Island to protect the southern approach to Charleston harbor, the fort could best be approached along a 60-yard-wide strip of land that limited attackers to one regiment at a time. After an eight-hour bombardment by Union artillery and naval ironclads failed to soften the Confederate defenses, the 54th launched its attack around 7:45 pm.

Their advance from the west brought them to within 150 yards of the fort before they came under heavy fire. Shaw's troops fought their way to the fort's parapet, where they engaged in hand-to-hand combat before being repulsed. The Union forces continued the fight until nearly 10:00 pm before withdrawing in defeat.

Thirty members of the 54th, including Colonel Shaw, were killed in action, and another 24 died later from wounds, while 15 were captured and 52 were reported missing and never seen again. The regiment's bravery, immortalized in the 1989 motion picture Glory, proved to be a boon to Union recruitment efforts among African Americans.

The 54th Massachusetts Colored Regiment charge at Fort Wagner.

in their service in a famous letter to his longtime friend, James Conkling. "Negroes, like other people, act upon motives. Why should they do anything for us," argued the president, "if we will do nothing for them? If they stake their lives for us, they must be prompted by the strongest motive—even the promise of freedom. And the promise being made, must be kept."

"The chattel is a man"

Once in the field, black troops faced perils far greater than their white comrades-in-arms. In December 1862, Confederate President Jefferson Davis ordered that captured black soldiers be turned over to state authorities, a potential death sentence because every Confederate state had laws calling for the execution of rebellious slaves. In July 1863, President Lincoln responded with an executive order vowing that "for every soldier of the United States killed in violation of the laws of war, a rebel soldier shall be executed; and for every one enslaved...a rebel soldier shall be placed

The 54th Massachusetts Colored Regiment march through Charleston, South Carolina.

The Fort Pillow Massacre

On April 12, 1864, a Confederate victory at Fort Pillow, situated along the Mississippi River

Soldiers battle at Fort Pillow.

40 miles north of Memphis, Tennessee, gave rise to one of the Civil War's most notorious incidents. About 10 am, the Union garrison of 600 men, evenly divided between black and white troops, came under attack by about 1,500 troops commanded by Nathan Bedford Forrest. Confederate artillery and sharpshooters kept up a steady fire until 3:30 pm, when Forrest asked the fort's commander to surrender. Major William F. Bradford's refusal led to a furious Confederate assault that quickly sent the Union defenders fleeing toward the Mississippi River, where hoped-for covering fire from a Union gunboat failed to materialize.

Most historians believe that between 4 pm and nightfall, Forrest's troops shot or bayoneted dozens of Union soldiers trying to surrender amid repeated cries of "No quarter! No quarter!" Estimated Union losses were 350 killed and mortally wounded, 60 wounded, and 164 captured or missing. Forrest lost 14 killed and 86 wounded. In the battle's aftermath, the Confederate command's refusal to guarantee that captured black troops would be treated as prisoners of war led to the suspension of prisoner exchanges. After considerable discussion, the Lincoln administration elected to take no retaliatory action.

at hard labor...until the other shall...receive the treatment due to a prisoner of war."

Although Lincoln's threat generally restrained Confederate treatment of black captives, it failed to prevent incidents such as the summary execution of dozens of black Union soldiers captured at Fort Pillow, Tennessee, in April 1864. This and similar grisly events ensured that black troops, knowing their likely fate if they surrendered, often fought with a sense of purpose and ferocity greater than many of their white comrades.

Members of the USCT also faced racism, inequality, and acts of discrimination from their own comrades. Union officers almost invariably assigned them to the nastiest camp duties. "Where white and black troops come together in the same command," noted General Lorenzo Thomas, "the latter have to do all the work." Black troops frequently received inferior food, clothing, and weaponry. Comparative mortality figures illustrate that black troops also received inferior medical care. In white regiments, nearly two soldiers died of disease for every one killed in battle; the comparable figure for black regiments was 10 soldiers killed by disease for every one slain on the battlefield. One in 12 white troops died of disease; one in five black troops did.

Black troops appeared willing to tolerate these many acts of discrimination in return for the promise of freedom and the chance to define their lives apart from slavery. As one white soldier observed, "Put a United States uniform on his back and the chattel is a man." But one issue did lead to a level of discontent that would threaten the effectiveness of black troops.

"A feeling of sullen distrust"

A white enlisted man was paid $13 a month (equivalent to about $240 today), an amount that included a clothing allowance of $3 to be spent at the soldier's discretion. Black troops received $10 a month, $3 of which was withheld for clothing. "Unequal pay," lamented Colonel Higginson, "has impaired discipline...and has begun to implant a feeling of sullen distrust."

This 1863 painting symbolically represents freedom for African Americans.

Secretary of War Stanton's promise of a pay equal to that received by white troops when the first black volunteers enlisted in the spring of 1863 was at the root of the problem. When told a few months later that the 1862 Militia Act clearly stated that "persons of African descent...shall receive ten dollars per month and one ration, three dollars of which monthly pay may be in clothing," Stanton was forced to backtrack. Efforts by Massachusetts and other state governments to make up the difference in pay met stiff resistance from the troops themselves. A spokesman for the 54th and 55th Massachusetts regiments condemned an offer for advertising "us to the world as holding out for money and not from principle." They were among many who refused time and again to muster to receive equal pay.

For many, the difference in pay represented more than principle. A soldier serving in the 8th USCT wrote that his "wife and three little children at home, are...freezing and starving to death. She writes to me for aid, but I have nothing to send her." When Frederick Douglass urged the president to address the issue during a White House meeting in August 1863, Lincoln was remarkably unmoved. Black troops, he argued, "had larger motives for being soldiers than white men" and "ought to be willing to enter the service upon any condition." Lower pay was a "necessary concession" that would ultimately be corrected.

In June 1864, Congress finally adopted legislation equalizing pay and making it retroactive to January 1. It also enabled black troops to collect back pay for 1862 and 1863, but hedged the entitlement with qualifications that spawned a whole new round of controversies that went unresolved until the war's end.

"The glory and the triumph of this hour"

The bravery and battlefield accomplishments of the USCT won over many of their white skeptics and were sources of great pride for newly freed African Americans. In no small irony, USCT regiments were among the first Federal troops to enter Charleston, flashpoint for the rebellion, and Richmond, capital of the Confederacy. "The glory and the triumph of this hour may be imagined, but can never be described," exulted Colonel Charles B. Fox when describing the entry of the 55th Massachusetts into Charleston on February 18, 1865. "The colored people turned out en masse." One Richmond resident recalled with dismay that as the Fifth Massachusetts Cavalry rode through the downtown streets, "our Richmond servants...danced and shouted, men hugged each other, and women kissed, and such a scene of confusion you have never seen."

After Lee's surrender at Appomattox, white soldiers were demobilized far more rapidly than their black comrades, who had enlisted for three-year terms of service beginning in mid-1863. Units of the USCT occupied 10 of the 11 Confederate states, with the greatest concentration in the lower Mississippi River Valley and the Atlantic coastal regions. From the outset, white Southerners resented the presence of the USCT and lodged consistent protests with Federal authorities. Although General Grant and other military leaders were generally supportive of the troops, the troops themselves were constantly harassed by Southern whites. In 1866, for example, riots in Columbus, Georgia, in February, Memphis in May, and New Orleans in July resulted in considerable loss of life and property damage.

Although garrison duty carried the constant threat of violence, boredom was also a feature of daily life. For many, this provided an opportunity to learn how to read and write. The long spells of inaction, however, sometimes led to frayed relationships between black soldiers and their white officers. Proud of their service and increasingly sensitive to inequities and slights, real and imagined, black troops on several occasions resisted the authority of senior officers. In 1866, a mutiny in Jacksonville, Florida, resulting from an overly harsh punishment was quickly put down and six of the participants were executed. Such incidents are noteworthy because they happened so rarely in an atmosphere that must have been very volatile.

Life for black veterans was not easy. One study found that black veterans were three times more likely to be unemployed than their white counterparts, and four times as likely to be jobless as black civilians. Veterans' groups provided minimal relief: the Grand Army of the Republic proved unwelcoming and allowed only segregated black units. After considerable debate, the regular peacetime army designated four infantry and two cavalry units as black. While service in the postwar military offered enlistees a guaranteed paycheck and an atmosphere that was somewhat less discriminatory than civilian life, fewer than 3,000 black Civil War veterans ever served in the postwar military.

Sadly, as time passed, the critical contributions of the black troops to the Union victory were increasingly minimized and denigrated by white veterans. By the 50th reunion of the Battle of Gettysburg in 1913, black veterans were all but invisible. Only during the past 30 years have historians restored the story of the USCT to its rightful place in the history of the American Civil War.

Black Soldiers in the Civil War

Not long after President Lincoln's Emancipation Proclamation, the Union army began recruiting African American soldiers into its ranks. By the end of the Civil War, roughly 179,000 black men (10 percent of the Union army) served as soldiers in the U.S. Army and another 19,000 served in the navy. Nearly 40,000 black soldiers died over the course of the war—30,000 of infection or disease. Black soldiers served in artillery and infantry, and black women, who could not formally join the army, nonetheless served as nurses, spies, and scouts.

The Veteran's Return, *by Tod Haskin Fredericks.*

Many African American soldiers were former slaves who had left their owners, but whether former slaves or free men, they faced prejudice, and early on were not used in combat. As they demonstrated the courage and willingness to fight, they were engaged more and more in combat. By the end of the war, 16 black soldiers had been awarded the Medal of Honor for their valor. To learn more about the Civil War and African American history, please visit www.nps.gov.